D0500705

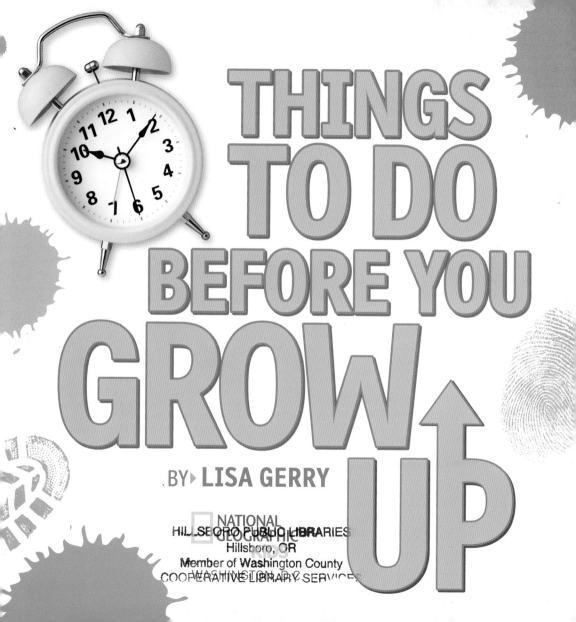

THINGS TO DO BEFORE YOU GROW UP

BY ▶ LISA GERRY

NATIONAL GEOGRAPHIC KIDS WASHINGTON, D.C.

FROM THE MOMENT YOU'RE BORN, THERE ARE ABOUT 6,570 DAYS BEFORE YOU'RE LEGALLY CONSIDERED AN ADULT.

That's it. From blocks to bank statements, pacifiers to parking tickets...it's not a lot of time. So, here's your mission, should you choose to accept it: Have as much fun, go on as many adventures, and do as much good as you possibly can in those 6,570 days. That's where this book comes in.

In your hands you hold more than 100 ideas for exciting adventures, silly escapades, and general life instructions for having fun, and, well, being a kid. There are lists and ideas, fun facts and how-to tips, and just in case you need help, there's even insight from awesome experts, explorers, and adventurers who've been in your shoes (and probably wish they were again). But it's not all jumping in leaves and baking cupcakes. In this book there are also challenges—challenges that will inspire you to face your fears, step out of your comfort zone, and be the best friend and neighbor you can be.

The goal of this book is to inspire you to make the most of every day and seize every opportunity. This is your time to explore, grow, be creative, and even make a difference. And, there's a bonus! With this fun-filled to-do list, you won't have to worry about being bored. The next time you think, I have nothing to do!, just pull out your list, flip to a page, and go for it. Check off the challenges in the back as you complete them, and if you think of other things you'd like to do, add to this list, or make a new one!

YOU'VE GOT A
FUN RIDE
AHEAD OF
YOU —so, buckle
up and have
a BLAST.

1

DO SOMETHING NICE
FOR SOMEONE BUT
DON'T TELL
THEM YOU DID IT

Did you know that being nice can actually make you feel better physically? Research shows it not only makes you more calm and relaxed, it can also ease pain, increase your energy, and help ease stomachaches!

6

2 LEARN A JOKE and HOW TO TELL IT

IT'S A REAL RUSH TO MAKE SOMEONE LAUGH— you've made them feel good and you feel good too. Laughing can create bonds between you and your friends, brighten bad days, and even make nerve-racking situations seem not all that scary. There are lots of different ways to perform comedy, like stand-up (standing in front of an audience and telling funny stories and/or jokes), improvisation (acting out make-believe scenarios with a group of people on the fly), or sketch comedy (writing short, funny scenes to perform for people).

PHYLLIS KATZ, A FOUNDING MEMBER OF THE GROUNDLINGS, an improvisation and sketch comedy theater and school in Los Angeles (where comedians like Will Ferrell, Kristen Wiig, and Melissa McCarthy trained), shares five tips for making people laugh.

1 DON'T BE AFRAID TO FAIL. "When you tell a joke, you're taking a risk that someone won't think it's funny. Everyone's afraid of looking foolish, but you have to be willing to take risks on stage. Taking a chance is how you make discoveries. And, the thing is, so what if you mess up? It's just a joke."

2 STAY IN THE MOMENT. "This applies to great improvisation and also to life. When you're feeling uncomfortable, your mind can jump to worrying about the future or the past. It will go everywhere but where it's supposed to be, which is right where you are. So, concentrate, stay in the moment, and let that moment take you to the next one."

3 BE BRAVE. "It's great to have self-confidence and it's important to respect yourself. But everybody's not confident all the time—we're human beings. So if you can't be confident, at least you can be brave. I am not someone who every time I get on stage thinks, Oh, I'm going to nail this! So, when I'm not feeling my most confident, I give myself points for bravery."

4 WATCH AND LEARN. "If you're interested in a particular kind of comedy, watch a lot of it, read books about it, take classes, learn the rules, and then try to find your own voice."

5 ENJOY YOURSELF! "You should have fun when you're telling a joke. Laughing feels good, and when you tell a joke, you're sharing that good feeling with someone else."

VISIT AN ORCHARD AND PICK YOUR OWN FRUIT

BONUS CHALLENGE:
Take it home and make a dessert for your family.

Apple trees take four to five years to produce their first fruit.

CLIMB
A MOUNTAIN

YOU DEFINITELY DON'T NEED TO CLIMB MOUNT EVEREST TO CROSS THIS ONE OFF YOUR LIST,

but Jordan Romero did! He broke the record for youngest person to climb Mount Everest—the highest mountain on Earth—when he was only 13! Jordan's journey began when he was 9 years old and noticed a mural in his elementary school hallway showing the "Seven Summits"—the highest mountains on each of the seven continents. He decided then that he wanted to climb to the top of every one of them—and he did! In fact, he is the youngest person to have ever done so. Now, at 17 years old, he is attempting to climb the highest peak in each of the 50 states (he's already completed 14!).

Jordan Romero

THE SEVEN SUMMITS

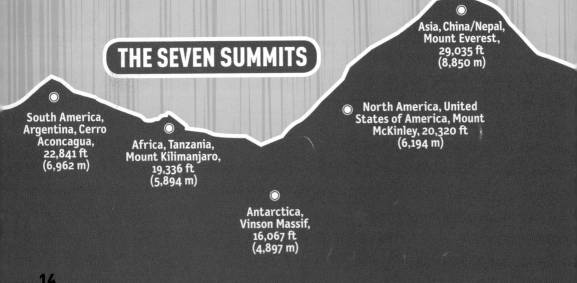

Asia, China/Nepal, Mount Everest, 29,035 ft (8,850 m)

South America, Argentina, Cerro Aconcagua, 22,841 ft (6,962 m)

Africa, Tanzania, Mount Kilimanjaro, 19,336 ft (5,894 m)

North America, United States of America, Mount McKinley, 20,320 ft (6,194 m)

Antarctica, Vinson Massif, 16,067 ft (4,897 m)

JORDAN'S FIVE FAVORITES:

BOOK: *No Shortcuts to the Top,* by Ed Viesturs. Viesturs climbed the 14 highest peaks in the world and is one of my inspirations.

MOVIE: The IMAX documentary *Everest.*

GEAR: For alpine mountaineering, the ice axe. It's a tool that has saved a lot of lives.

PART OF THE CLIMB: Reaching the summit. Mountain climbing can be slow. There's a lot of pushing through nasty weather and walking uphill. But when you finally get to the top, it's the best feeling ever.

PHILOSOPHY: Always cherish the moment.

Europe, Russia,
Mount Elbrus,
18,510 ft
(5,642 m)

Australia/Oceania,
Indonesia, Mount
Carstensz Pyramid,
16,024 ft
(4,884 m)

RIDE A
ROLLER
COASTER

17

6

BECOME A PEN PAL

BY AIR MAIL
PAR AVION

Some mail carriers had a much longer route than they do today. In 1860, the Pony Express began carrying mail by horseback from St. Joseph, Missouri, to Sacramento, California—a trip of more than 1,800 miles (2,897 km), which on average took ten days.

COMMUNICATE WITH A FARAWAY FRIEND VIA SNAIL MAIL, NOT EMAIL.

7

TRY YOGA

Laughter yoga is a type of yoga where participants make themselves laugh in order to reap its benefits, including better mood, less anxiety, improved immune system, relaxation, and better sleep.

IN 2012, RESEARCHERS AT THE UNIVERSITY OF ILLINOIS FOUND THAT AFTER 20 MINUTES OF YOGA, students' memory and mental performance improved. So, while you might not be ready to bend into a human pretzel, why not give it a whirl and start small? Here's a simple pose to get you started:

Proven benefits of yoga include:

Better sleep

Improved flexibility

Stress reduction

Improved mood

Increased muscle strength

TREE POSE

1 Begin by standing with your feet apart and lift one leg.

2 Place that leg above or below your knee on the other leg, which you want to keep planted firmly into the ground (like a tree trunk).

3 Stand tall, lifting your torso and extending your arms to the sky (like tree branches).

4 Breathe in and out.

5 For extra fun (and if you're feeling brave), do your best tree impression and move your arms like branches in the wind, or hold hands with another "tree" to make a forest.

RAKE LEAVES
INTO A BIG PILE AND THEN
JUMP
IN THEM

PERSUADE YOUR PARENTS TO MAKE A CHANGE FOR THE ENVIRONMENT

Here are 10 quick, easy changes that could have a big impact.

1 Eat a vegetarian dinner one night a week.

2 Bring reusable bags to the grocery store.

3 Cut down on your time in the shower.

4 Reduce the amount of wasted paper by unsubscribing to junk mail.

5 Choose reusable water bottles instead of disposable plastic.

6 Challenge family members to put a quarter in a jar every time they leave a room with the light on.

7 Replace all the lightbulbs in the house with the more energy-efficient LED bulbs.

8 Whenever you can, walk instead of riding in a car.

9 Recycle.

10 Start a compost pile.

10

RECORD YOUR DREAMS FOR A WEEK

Then try to decode them to discover what's going on in your brain when you sleep.

Everyone dreams, but not everyone remembers their dreams. You're most likely to remember dreams when you wake up during or shortly thereafter them.

5 POPULAR DREAM THEMES AND WHAT THEY MIGHT MEAN

Monsters can be pretty scary and threatening, so this dream might mean that there's someone or something that's been making you feel that way in real life.

Not knowing your way may indicate that you're unsure about a decision you need to make.

FLYING

Flying often symbolizes freedom, so this dream may point to your desire to have a bit more flexibility and/or independence in your daily routine.

SOMEONE FAMOUS

If famous people appear in your dream, they may have some positive traits that you admire or wish you had more of (or, maybe you're just watching too much TV).

BEING CHASED

If you dream that you are trying to outrun someone or something, perhaps you're feeling intimidated or that you're unable to escape something that is making you feel anxious.

GO CAMPING

CAMPING TO-DO LIST

1 Sleep under the STARS.

2 Tell SCARY STORIES with a flashlight.

3 Try to identify an ANIMAL TRACK.

4 SING SONGS around a campfire.

5 Make S'MORES.

S'MORES

½ Graham cracker

½ Graham cracker

½ Chocolate bar

Toasted marshmallow

RIDE A HORSE

Most wild horses are descendants of horses that were once tame and then ran away. The Przewalski's horse is the only truly wild horse whose ancestors were never domesticated.

13 BECOME AN EXPERT AT SOMETHING

IT CAN BE USEFUL KNOWING A LITTLE BIT ABOUT A LOT OF THINGS, BUT IT'S ALSO REALLY COOL TO KNOW A LOT ABOUT ONE THING. Even if no one else has heard of what you're into, knowing the ins and outs of a single subject shows that you're passionate. Plus it's sure to come in handy— there will be no need for Googling when you're around! So, what do you find really interesting? Superheroes, cupcakes, dinosaurs, sewing, history, soccer, video games … it can be anything!

→ Find out everything there is to know about that subject.

→ Find people who know even more than you do, ask questions, and listen. There's always more to be learned from fellow experts.

→ To become an expert, you have to spend a lot of time thinking about, and doing work in, a single subject area. So, make sure this is something you're really interested in, be dedicated, and don't give up.

→ Don't be afraid to mess up. Sometimes the greatest discoveries come on the heels of big mistakes.

14

OF YOUR

STEP OUTSIDE

TRY TASTING A NEW FOOD (think kale, star fruit, or escargot)! TALK TO SOMEONE YOU'VE NEVER MET (maybe you'll make a new friend)! EXPLORE SOMEWHERE YOU'VE NEVER BEEN (even just a new neighborhood)! You'll never know what you're truly capable of until you push beyond your boundaries a little bit.

COMFORT ZONE

15

RUN A 5K

WHY? BECAUSE IT'S GOOD FOR YOU, IT'S FUN, AND YOU'LL FEEL LIKE A ROCK STAR WHEN YOU'RE DONE!

Running is something you can do for the rest of your life," says Dr. Joel Brenner, Chair of the American Academy of Pediatrics' Council on Sports Medicine and Fitness. "Anyone can do it and you can do it anywhere. The only equipment you need is a pair of shoes." And, bonus! People who run, he says, experience better moods, more energy, better concentration at school, and increased confidence and self-esteem. If you choose to run with other people, running can also be a great way to make friends and be part of a team.

WITH PROPER TRAINING, A FIVE-KILOMETER RUN (WHICH IS ABOUT 3.1 MILES) IS A GREAT PLACE TO START. HERE ARE FIVE TIPS FROM DR. BRENNER ON HOW TO GET STARTED AND DO IT RIGHT.

1 **VISIT YOUR DOCTOR.** Before you get started, go to your pediatrician for a checkup. He or she will screen for any medical problems that could interfere with sports participation or physical activity.

2 GET THE RIGHT SHOES. There are three types of feet, those that overpronate (roll in too much), those that underpronate (roll out too much), and those that are neutral and do neither. Wearing the wrong shoes can lead to injuries, so it's important to have ones best suited for your foot type. To find out the best shoe for your feet, you can visit a sports medicine physician or a specialty running store, or check out resources online.

3 TRAIN! START BY WALKING AND JOGGING. To begin, try completing a mile. If you've never run before, you might walk the whole mile, or you might walk one minute, run one minute, alternating until you reach a mile. Then, increase your weekly mileage by no more than 10 percent (For example, if you're running 10 miles total in a week, the next week you can increase it to 11). Take at least one day off from training per week and on those days, try a different type of physical activity.

4 DO A TRIAL RUN. Don't wear a brand-new pair of shoes on the day of the race. In fact, make sure you've run in them for a few weeks. Decide what you're going to eat before your race and what outfit you're going to wear, then have a trial run. Make sure your stomach feels good and that you feel comfortable.

5 Be sure to DRINK ENOUGH WATER and then, HAVE FUN!

16

HELP
SOMEONE
IN NEED

Looking for ideas? You could ...

- Sit with someone at lunch who's sitting alone.
- Bring an extra pen or pencil to a test, then lend it to someone who forgot his.
- Introduce yourself to the new kid in class.
- Offer to walk a busy neighbor's dog.
- Help your teacher put the chairs up after class.
- Stick up for someone being bullied.
- Volunteer to bring a sick student her homework.
- Be a good listener to a friend going through a tough time.
- Share your lunch with someone who forgot to bring it.

HERE ARE FIVE MUST-DO MUD ACTIVITIES:

1. Walk barefoot.
2. Make a mudslide.
3. Search for worms.
4. Create mud bricks.
(Fill an old ice cube tray with mud and let it dry in the sun. Then build something cool!)
5. Go for a mud run.

17

PLAY IN THE MUD

Before every game, the balls used in Major League Baseball are rubbed in mud packaged from the Delaware River to remove their sheen and make them easier to grip.

18 LEARN TO PLAY AN INSTRUMENT

Then put out a tip jar and give an impromptu performance for your family, neighbors, and friends.

Most of the bows used to play stringed instruments (like the violin, viola, cello, and bass) are made from hair taken from a horse's tail.

19

TRY ANOTHER COUNTRY'S CUISINE

Snacks in other countries vary just as much as main meals. If you were a kid in Japan, you might snack on sardine rice crackers at the movies. In Canada—forget ketchup! French fries are smothered in poutine, a mixture of gravy and cheese curds. And in Mexico, a mango lollipop covered in chili paste called Vero Mango is a favorite treat!

CHEW ON THIS
make your own SUSHI!

 1 Make 1½ cups of sushi rice according to package directions. Have a parent help cut 1 cucumber into several matchstick-size slices, then thinly slice 1 avocado and grate 1 carrot.

 2 Mix 2 tablespoons of rice wine vinegar and 1 tablespoon of sugar and microwave for 30 seconds. Stir to dissolve the sugar. In a large bowl, stir the rice and slowly add the vinegar mixture.

 3 Place 1 seaweed sheet, shiny-side down, on a sushi mat. Spread ¾ cup of the rice over the seaweed sheet, leaving a small empty strip at one of the shorter ends.

 4 Spread 2 teaspoons of mayonnaise over the center of the rice. Top with a small handful of cucumber, avocado, and carrot slices.

 5 Using the sushi mat, roll up firmly to form a roll. Cut into 6 slices. Repeat to make 24 pieces. Serve with wasabi and ginger.

20

The world record for most swing dance flips in a minute is 39 and was achieved by Lourd Vijay, of India. He needed help from three different dance partners to break the record.

LEARN A DANCE

21

VOLUNTEER IN YOUR COMMUNITY

VOLUNTEERING WON'T JUST MAKE YOU FEEL GREAT, the work you do can better the lives of people and animals, as well as help the environment in a big way. "Kids see things in their community that they're concerned about, like animals that are hungry or children at school who don't have a coat," says Wendy Spencer, CEO of the Corporation for National and Community Service. "Volunteering is something that you can do to address a problem that you see firsthand. By volunteering, you can actually make a difference and change the world as you see it."

WENDY SHARES THE FOLLOWING TIPS FOR HOW YOU CAN GET INVOLVED:

• **FIND SOMETHING YOU CARE ABOUT.** Is there a problem you've seen that you want to address? You're more likely to enjoy your experience if you're passionate about the cause.

• **MAKE IT FUN.** Bring along a buddy, sibling, parent, or grandparent so that you enjoy the time you spend helping others.

• **INVITE SOMEONE NEW ALONG.** If there's a new student in your school, or kid in your neighborhood, a great way to help them to make friends and get more comfortable is to invite them to join you while you're volunteering.

• **VOLUNTEER WITH A TEAM.** If you're already a member of a club or sports team, volunteer together as a group. There will be more people to help and it will give everyone a sense of pride.

• **CONSIDER YOUR TALENTS.** When considering how you can help, get your friends, family, and neighbors together and think about what unique talents or resources you all have that could be of use. Does someone's parent have a truck you could use to haul supplies? Do you have a friendly pet that you could bring to a hospital or nursing home to cheer people up? Do you have canned goods or coats that you could donate to a good cause?

• **ASK HOW YOU CAN HELP.** If you're not sure the best way to help, ask a teacher, parent, coach, or other trusted adult what problems they see in your community and how you could help.

ADOPT
AN ANIMAL

AFTER MONTHS OF PLEADING and convincing the powers that be that **YOU'RE READY TO HAVE A PET**, you've finally been **GIVEN THE OK.** You're going to have a **NEW FURRY FRIEND** all your own. **SO, WHAT NEXT?**

> The domestic dogs that we keep as pets today evolved from wild wolves.

Dr. Gary Weitzman, president and CEO of the San Diego SPCA and cohost of the nationally distributed public radio program *The Animal House* says your next move should be to make a visit to your local animal shelter. "There are three to four million homeless animals in America that won't find their way into homes," he says. "Part of being a good, responsible pet parent is being responsible in how you acquire your pet."

HERE, GARY EXPLAINS HOW TO MAKE YOUR NEW PET FEEL RIGHT AT HOME.

STEP 1: Before adopting an animal, be sure that you're able to care for its three basic needs: housing, food, and enrichment (behavioral training, toys, and active play).

STEP 2: Meet with an adoption counselor at your local shelter to see which type and breed of animal is best suited for you.

STEP 3: Be prepared. Most shelters will give you a list of items you'll need to take care of your new pet. Also, your pet is going to need quality time with you during the first few weeks so that there is an instant bond, so consider adopting during summer vacation or over a holiday.

If you can't adopt an animal ... there are still lots of ways to help care for one. Call your local shelter and ask about volunteer opportunities. You could also ask if there are specific items the shelter needs and start a collection at your school, or organize a bake sale to raise funds.

23

READ AN ENTIRE BOOK SERIES

HERE ARE FIVE GREAT SERIES WORTH READING:

Sea of Trolls, by Nancy Farmer

His Dark Materials, by Philip Pullman

Artemis Fowl, by Eoin Colfer

Percy Jackson & the Olympians, by Rick Riordan

Harry Potter, by J. K. Rowling

MAKE HOMEMADE ICE CREAM

"Balboa Island, California, is famous for its chocolate-covered frozen bananas, dipped in sprinkles and nuts," says Food Network chef Melissa d'Arabian. "Summertime lines at banana stands are filled with both tourists and locals stopping by for this iconic treat. This ice-cream recipe celebrates all the flavors that remind me of my own childhood devouring Balboa bananas. And now, I've gotten my husband and four daughters hooked on them too!"

24

Dolley Madison, who was married to the fifth president of the United States, James Madison, was a huge fan of ice cream and would often make it in the White House. Her favorite flavor? Oyster!

BALBOA BANANA ICE CREAM
Recipe courtesy of Melissa d'Arabian

Melissa d'Arabian

YIELD: 5 servings
TOTAL PREP TIME: About 4 hours, including custard chill time and ice cream freezing
EASE OF PREPARATION: Intermediate

CUSTARD:
5 egg yolks
1 cup milk
¼ teaspoon table salt
¼ cup sugar
2 tablespoons corn syrup

BANANA CREAM:
2 medium bananas, peeled, sliced, and frozen
1/2 cup heavy cream
2 teaspoons vanilla

MIX-INS:
3 tablespoons rainbow sprinkles
3 tablespoons chopped nuts (peanuts, almonds, pecans)
¼ cup chocolate chips
1 tablespoon heavy cream

WHILE YOU MAKE THE CUSTARD, chill a medium metal bowl in the freezer. In another medium bowl, use a fork to mix the yolks and set aside.

HEAT THE MILK IN A HEAVY SAUCEPAN OVER MEDIUM HEAT, stirring frequently with a wooden spoon, until the milk begins to steam (do not boil). Once the milk is hot, temper the yolks: Pour a spoonful of hot milk into the yolks while mixing with a fork. Add another ounce or so of milk to the yolks, stirring. Then, pour the yolk and milk mixture into the pan of milk, while stirring. Add the salt, sugar, and corn syrup, and heat over medium heat, stirring almost constantly, until the mixture thickens enough to coat the back of the spoon, about 3 to 5 minutes. If the mixture begins to boil, lower the heat. Once the custard is thick, pour into a bowl and cover with plastic wrap, with the wrap touching the surface of the custard. Chill for at least 2 hours.

ONCE THE CUSTARD IS CHILLED, make the banana cream. In a food processor, mix the frozen bananas, cream, and vanilla together until creamy with a few small chunks remaining, about 15 seconds. Do not let the mixture get soupy; it should be the consistency of very soft soft-serve ice cream. Scrape the banana cream into the chilled metal bowl and freeze briefly, just to firm up the texture, about 10 to 15 minutes.

REMOVE THE BANANA CREAM FROM THE FREEZER, and using a hand mixer on low speed, combine the custard with the banana cream in the metal bowl. Mix just until homogeneous; don't let it get soupy. Do first full freeze of 30 to 45 minutes.

AFTER FIRST FULL FREEZE, remove the metal bowl from the freezer. The mixture will be harder and icier on the edges and bottom of the bowl, and softer and fluffier in the middle. Mix with a hand mixer on low until the entire mixture is creamy. Work quickly, and don't let the ice cream get soupy. Return the bowl to the freezer for second full freeze of 30 to 45 minutes.

ABOUT FIVE MINUTES BEFORE THE SECOND FULL FREEZE IS DONE, prepare the mix-ins: Measure out the sprinkles and chopped nuts. Melt the chocolate chips and cream in a small bowl in the microwave until smooth, stirring and checking every 15 seconds.

REMOVE THE BOWL FROM THE FREEZER, and stir in the nuts and the sprinkles with a wooden spoon or rubber spatula. Smooth the ice cream so it lays flat at the bottom of the bowl. Use a teaspoon to drizzle in the chocolate in fine lines across the ice cream in random directions. Note: You may have to reheat the sauce a few seconds in the microwave to keep it thin enough to drizzle. Work quickly, as you don't want the warm sauce to melt the ice cream. Once the ice cream is covered with chocolate drizzle, return the bowl to the freezer for the third and final full freeze of 30 to 45 minutes.

AFTER THE FINAL FREEZE, remove the bowl, and stir the ice cream, breaking up the chocolate into the ice cream. Serve immediately, or keep in the freezer up to 5 days. If storing in the freezer, let the ice cream sit at room temperature for 5 minutes before serving.

25

GO TO A CONCERT

The concert venues on Katy Perry's "California Dreams" tour were infused with the scent of cotton candy.

26 LEARN HOW TO SEW

ON A
BUTTON

Buttons are made from all kinds of materials, including animal bone, bamboo, glass, seashells, and even coconut shells.

THERE ARE SEVERAL WAYS TO SEW ON A BUTTON.

HERE ARE EASY STEP-BY-STEP INSTRUCTIONS FOR FLAT BUTTONS WITH TWO HOLES:

STEP 1
Slide a piece of thread through the eye of the needle so that the length is equal on either side. Then, tie the ends together in a knot.

STEP 2
Put the button in the appropriate spot on your piece of clothing. (Make sure it lines up properly with the buttonhole.)

STEP 3
Push the threaded needle up from the back of the fabric, through one of the holes in the button.

STEP 4
Push the needle down through the next hole, through the fabric, and then pull the thread all the way until it stops at the knot.

STEP 5
Bring the needle and thread up through the first hole again.

STEP 6
Repeat steps 3 through 5 until the button is securely fastened to the fabric.

STEP 7
On the last stitch, push the needle through the fabric without putting it through one of the button's holes.

STEP 8
Pull the thread out between the button and the fabric. Then, wrap the thread six times around the thread that is between the button and the fabric to create what is called a shank.

STEP 9
Push the needle through to the backside of the fabric, make one stitch in the back, then tie the thread into a tight knot.

STEP 10
Cut off the excess thread. Pat yourself on the back for a job well done!

27

CATCH A

Many common species
of fish change from male
to female, or vice versa,
during their lifetime.

FISH

(AND BE SURE TO TAKE A PICTURE!)

28

GO TO A PARADE

BETTER YET—
BE IN ONE OR
START YOUR OWN!

Write a Letter
TO MAKE A
DIFFERENCE

You may not be old enough to vote yet, but you're definitely old enough to express your opinions and create positive change. So, no need to sulk about the lack of dog parks in your town, or the fact that the baseball field doesn't have lights so that you can play at night. Do something about it! If you see something going on that you think is wrong, or could use improving, write a letter to one of your local leaders.

HERE ARE SOME TIPS from Naomi Hirabayashi at DoSomething.org on how to write the best, most effective letter possible.

• Keep your letter SHORT and to the point.

• Explain why you're writing, the problem you see, and POSSIBLE SOLUTIONS to that problem.

• Explain how your suggested solutions would BENEFIT THEM and THE COMMUNITY.

• Be POLITE and RESPECTFUL.

• Briefly explain WHY this issue is personally IMPORTANT TO YOU, but also include facts to back up your feelings.

• Include your name, address, and ways to contact you (phone number, email address) on the letter and the envelope.

Some of the world's fastest trains don't have wheels. Instead, they use a technology called magnetic levitation and actually float above their tracks and are propelled by magnetic force.

TO-DO LIST
- ☑ FLY IN A PLANE
- ☑ BOARD A TRAIN
- ☑ TAKE A HELICOPTER
- ☑ RIDE IN A BOAT
- ☑ SKATEBOARD

SAVE

ENOUGH MONEY
TO BUY $OMETHING YOU'VE HAD
YOUR EYE ON

Fourteen-year-old Willow Tufano, from Florida, saved enough money by reselling various items, such as discarded furniture from foreclosed homes, to buy a whole house with her mom.

THROW A
BACKYARD

BASH

CAN'T GO TO THE CARNIVAL?

BRING THE CARNIVAL TO YOU!

Invite your friends and neighbors over for an afternoon of outdoor fun. Here are five easy DIY ideas for backyard games.

+ = **BOWLING**

Gather up empty plastic water bottles and use them as pins. Then designate a line for people to stand behind and roll a rubber or plastic ball, about the size of a bowling ball. (Tip: If the wind is knocking the bottles over, fill them with water and use a heavier ball.)

WATER GUN TARGET PRACTICE

Balance plastic Ping-Pong balls on top of empty plastic bottles. Whoever can shoot the most balls off of the top of the bottles with a water gun wins!

BEAN BAG TOSS

Draw a face (like an animal, human, or clown) on a piece of poster board, cut out a large mouth, then prop it up against two chairs and have friends toss bean bags (or snack bags filled with rice or beans) through the hole.

THE AIM GAME

Stack cans into a pyramid on top of a table, box, or barrel, then have people throw a tennis ball or softball and see how many they can knock down.

RING TOSS

Gather enough plastic or glass bottles to fit, side by side, in a shallow cardboard box. Then have guests stand back and toss three rings (or rolls of tape) to see how many they can get around the bottles.

33

Bamboo is the fastest growing plant in the world. It can grow up to almost three feet (0.9 m) in a single day!

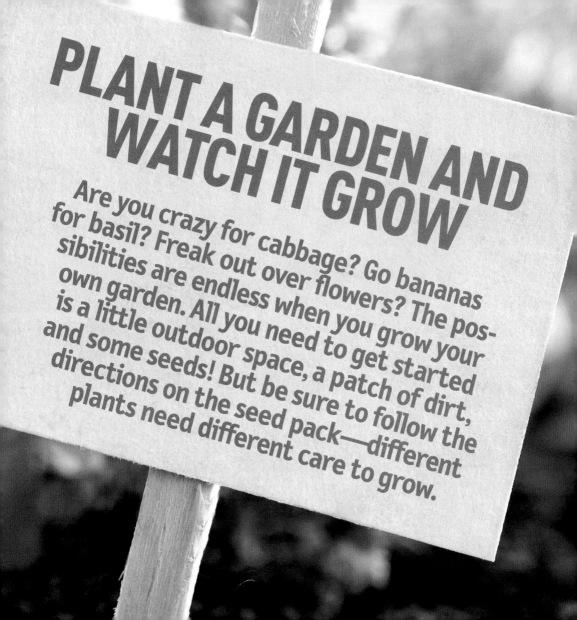

PLANT A GARDEN AND WATCH IT GROW

Are you crazy for cabbage? Go bananas for basil? Freak out over flowers? The possibilities are endless when you grow your own garden. All you need to get started is a little outdoor space, a patch of dirt, and some seeds! But be sure to follow the directions on the seed pack—different plants need different care to grow.

The game of basketball was invented by James Naismith, a physical education teacher at a small Massachusetts college, to keep a rowdy group of students busy and the football players in shape during the off-season. It was originally played using a soccer ball and woven peach baskets.

35

RIDE YOUR BIKE SOMEWHERE THAT YOU'D USUALLY TAKE A CAR

In Amsterdam, the population is 800,000, but there are 880,000 bicycles—four times the number of cars.

BLOW

BUBBLES

SWIM

IN AN OCEAN, LAKE, OR STREAM

TO REALLY CARE ABOUT SOMETHING AND BE PASSIONATE ABOUT IT, you first have to understand it," says Katy Croff Bell, National Geographic explorer and oceanographer. "Swimming is the first step to knowing and really understanding the water and the ocean. Growing up, I did all sorts of water activities—sailing, water skiing, surfing, scuba diving. It's how I developed a love of being in and around the water.

AN INTERVIEW WITH
Katy Croff Bell

Katy Croff Bell

Q: What is it that you do?
A: I use advanced technologies to explore the ocean.

Q: What are you looking for?
A: Anything that is previously undiscovered, including new species of organisms, volcanoes, and archaeological sites like shipwrecks. My job incorporates chemistry, biology, archaeology, engineering, and geology.

Q: What's your favorite part of what you do?
A: Having the opportunity to explore what we don't know about our planet and sharing it with anybody in the world.

Q: What do you find fascinating about the ocean?
A: We know so little about it and there are so many opportunities for exploration and discovery—especially for young explorers.

KATY'S FIVE FAVORITES:

PLACE TO SWIM: Anywhere I can find some water. A pool, lake, beach, river—wherever.

UNDERWATER CREATURE: Octopuses are really cool to find. They can camouflage and are incredibly smart.

SWIMMING MEMORY: Learning to scuba dive. It's incredible because you can stay underwater for so much longer and you actually feel like you're part of this very foreign environment. One of my favorite places to dive is the kelp beds in San Diego; it feels like you are swimming in an underwater forest.

GAME TO PLAY IN THE WATER: Greased watermelon water polo. You have two teams and a goal on each side of the pool, like soccer. Then, you coat a watermelon with Vaseline or Crisco and try to get it through the opposite team's goal. It is so funny.

UNDERWATER DISCOVERY: The one we haven't made yet.

American swimmer Michael Phelps competed in his first Olympic games when he was 15 years old. Twelve years later, in 2012, he set the record for most medals won by an Olympic athlete, with 22 medals (18 gold, 2 silver, and 2 bronze).

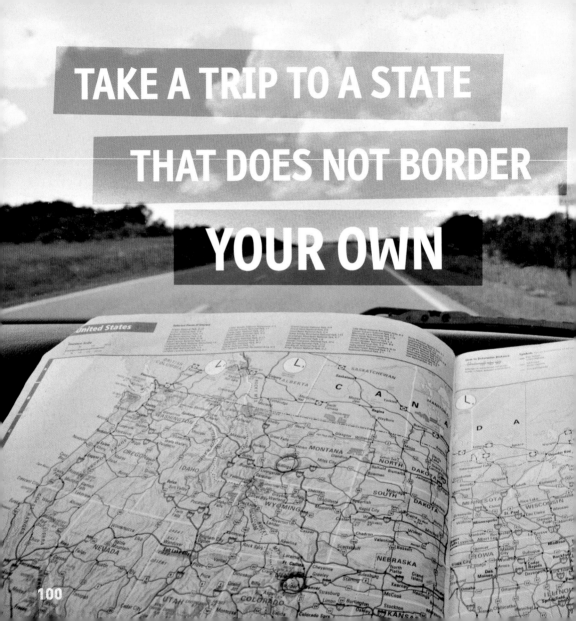

TAKE A TRIP TO A STATE

THAT DOES NOT BORDER

YOUR OWN

100

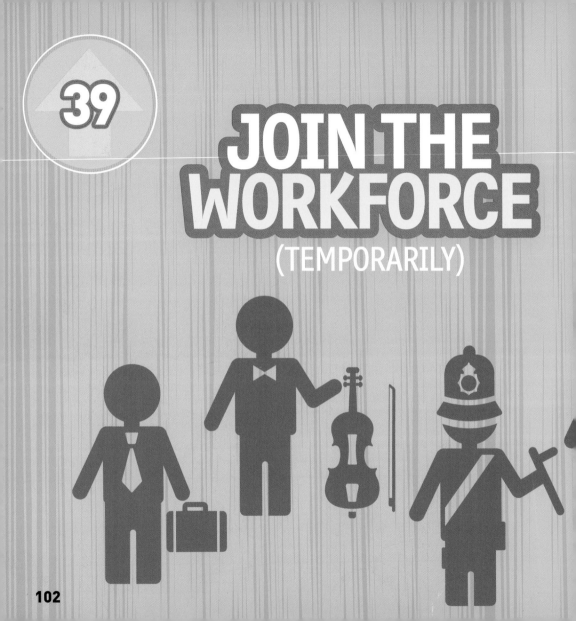

39

JOIN THE WORKFORCE
(TEMPORARILY)

Find an adult who has a job you think is awesome, then shadow him or her for a day. TAKE NOTES and ASK QUESTIONS. WHO KNOWS? You might DISCOVER YOUR DESTINY.

40

BECOME A MASTER PUBLIC SPEAKER

When Martin Luther King, Jr., wrote his "I Have a Dream" speech, he didn't include that famous phrase— he improvised it in the moment.

DOES THE THOUGHT OF GOING TO A DENTIST SOUND MORE APPEALING THAN GIVING A ONE-MINUTE SPEECH?

Even if the idea of taking the mic makes your hands sweat and your heart beat fast, you may be an ace presenter and not even know it. All it takes is a little practice and knowing how to prepare.

Public speaking is the most important asset someone can have today," says Jess Teutonico, curator of TEDx-Teen, an independently organized TED event. "It helps to hone your confidence and communication skills.

HERE, JESS SHARES THE FOUR ELEMENTS OF A GREAT SPEECH:

BE YOURSELF.

The most important thing about public speaking is that your personality shines through. To do that, just be real. If you're naturally bubbly, be bubbly. If you're shy, don't try to be extroverted. Don't wear uncomfortable clothes, too much makeup, or do your hair differently. You'll feel most confident and powerful when you're true to yourself.

PREPARATION, PREPARATION, PREPARATION.

Don't limit your rehearsals to one location. Practice in every corner of your room, inside, outside, wearing different clothes, and in front of various family and friends. The more you vary how you practice, the more comfortable you'll feel on the actual day.

TREAT YOUR SPEECH LIKE A PLAY.

Think about what you want the audience to take away from your speech, then write it accordingly. Add drama to the beginning, middle, and end. Your first line should do more than introduce you, it should grab people's attention. Halfway through your speech, you should have a moment of surprise, something that makes the listeners' jaws drop. Then, end your speech with an action item or a high-impact, compelling statement.

PRETEND YOU'RE TALKING TO A FRIEND.

Sometimes when speakers get on stage, they get very stiff and rigid, but the best way to get through to people is if you're real, like you're sitting down and chatting with them. Don't try to impress, try to communicate and inspire.

READY TO SHOW OFF YOUR PUBLIC SPEAKING SKILLS?

CHECK OUT THE TEDxTeen WEBSITE and apply to be a speaker at their next conference. Or, challenge a sibling or friend to a contest. Write a persuasive speech on what you want for dinner. Present both speeches to a parent and the most persuasive one wins!

41

Learn how to
scramble an egg, make a grilled cheese sandwich, and ice a cake

THREE BASIC SKILLS THAT WILL IMPRESS **ANYONE!**

HOW TO
SCRAMBLE
AN EGG:

STEP 1: Crack 2 eggs per person into a bowl, being careful not to get any bits of shell inside the bowl. (If you see some floating around, get them out with a fork. You could use your finger, but wash your hands thoroughly both before and after.)

STEP 2: Add a splash of milk or water and a dash of salt and pepper (to taste).

STEP 3: Briskly beat the mixture together with a whisk or fork until the egg whites and yolks have combined and the mixture is solid yellow.

STEP 4: Heat about 2 teaspoons of butter in a skillet on the stove over low heat and use the handle to tip the pan, allowing the butter to coat the bottom as it melts.

STEP 5: Pour the egg mixture into the skillet and continuously move it around the bottom with a spatula until it's firm and there are no more wet parts.

STEP 6: Remove the eggs with the spatula and put them on a plate. Enjoy!

HOW TO MAKE A GRILLED CHEESE:

STEP 1: Put 1 or 2 slices of American cheese between 2 pieces of bread.

STEP 2: Butter both sides of your sandwich, making sure to get butter all the way to the edges (unbuttered parts will quickly burn).

STEP 3: Turn the stove on medium heat and coat the bottom of a skillet with nonstick cooking spray.

STEP 4: When the stove is hot, place your sandwich in the center of the skillet and allow it to cook until that side is golden brown (about a minute and a half).

STEP 5: Flip the sandwich over, allowing the other side to cook until it's golden brown (this side will cook faster).

STEP 6: Take your sandwich off the stove, let it cool, and enjoy!

HOW TO ICE A CAKE:

STEP 1: First, let the cake cool completely.
(The hardest part is resisting the urge to dig in right away!)

STEP 2: Brush off any loose crumbs or bits of cake from the surface.

STEP 3: Spoon half of the frosting onto the top of the cake, in the center.

STEP 4: Using a knife or small metal spatula, spread the frosting toward the edges of the cake and eventually over the sides.

STEP 5: Wait 15 minutes and repeat steps 3 and 4 with a second coating of frosting.

STEP 6: To avoid getting crumbs mixed into the frosting, wipe your knife off before dipping it back into the frosting bowl and make sure you have plenty of frosting on your knife at all times.

42

POW!

MAKE YOUR OWN
COMIC
BOOK

BANG!

BOOM

When Stan Lee first created the Incredible Hulk in 1962, he was gray. But due to problems printing the gray color consistently, after the first comic book was published, they made him green.

GIVE IT A COOL TITLE, LIKE ...
"THE AWESOME LIFE OF LADY LIONHEART"

NEED HELP COMING UP WITH A SUPERHERO NAME?
Pick one word from column A and one from column B.
Now you can start writing your first adventure!

COLUMN A	COLUMN B
Mighty	Kid
Brave	Warrior
Mega	Hero
Awesome	Conqueror
Magnificent	Avenger
Spectacular	Champion
Magical	Crusader
Gutsy	Friend
Tremendous	Guardian
Wicked	Wizard

43

VISIT A WORKING

WORKING

TO-DO LIST

- ☑ TOUR THE GROUNDS
- ☑ MILK A COW
- ☑ COLLECT EGGS
- ☑ FEED A GOAT OR PIG
- ☑ BRUSH A HORSE

FARM

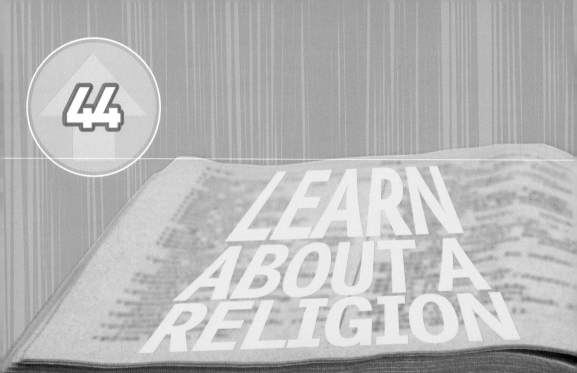

44

LEARN ABOUT A RELIGION

Not sure how to get started?

OTHER THAN YOUR OWN

Ask a friend or family member if you can tag along to their next worship service.

45

Write
A POEM

NEED SOME INSPIRATION? READ THIS POEM BY FORMER
U.S. CHILDREN'S POET LAUREATE J. PATRICK LEWIS.

KEEP A POCKET IN YOUR POEM
By J. Patrick Lewis

Based off the poem
"Keep a poem in your pocket."
Beatrice Schenk de Regniers

Keep a pocket in your poem
Filled with any wondrous thing
You can think of—red hawk feather,
Silver penny, pinkie ring,

Yo-yo, M&M's, a ticket
To a rollercoaster ride,
Pictures of your pug. A poem
Needs a pocket on the side.

So—
Keep a pocket in your poem
For imagination grows
From the deepest secret pockets
Every pocket poet knows.

The first poet to ever recite a poem at a U.S. president's inauguration was Robert Frost in 1961 at John F. Kennedy, Jr.'s inauguration.

119

WATCH A BLACK-AND-WHITE MOVIE

46

5 AWESOME FACTS ABOUT BLACK-AND-WHITE MOVIES

1 The first public showing of a motion picture was in 1891 and it featured William Dickson, the man who created the first motor-powered camera, bowing, smiling and taking off his hat.

2 The first movie theater opened in Paris, France, in 1895.

3 The first female-directed film was made in Paris in 1896 by Alice Guy-Blaché. It was a one-minute-long fictional film called *La Fée aux Choux (The Cabbage Fairy)*.

4 In the early 1900s, movie theaters called "nickel-odeons" began to pop up around America. The name came from the price of admission—one nickel.

5 Filmmakers originally moved to Los Angeles in the early 1900s in search of sunshine, because there were no ways yet to artificially light film sets.

47

CHAMPION A CAUSE
YOU CARE ABOUT

An Interview With
UNDERWATER PHOTOJOURNALIST
BRIAN SKERRY

Q: When did you know what you wanted to be when you grew up?
A: I became a certified scuba diver when I was 14 and a year later I attended a conference with underwater filmmakers and photographers. I had somewhat of an epiphany. It occurred to me that this was the perfect career for me—I could be an ocean explorer, but with a camera. I could tell stories visually, as a way of exploring the seas.

Q: What is the most thrilling part of working underwater?
A: That the ocean remains largely unknown, and on any given day, when you slip your head beneath the waves, you never know quite what you're going to find.

Q: What do you hope people learn about the ocean through your photographs?
A: That the ocean is somewhat fragile and we have to be cautious about how we treat it. Also, I would hope that people understand from my work how beautiful and important the ocean is to all of our lives, regardless of where we live.

Q: What have you learned from your ocean conservation efforts?
A: I've learned that people do care and we can make a difference. It may sometimes seem like a daunting task—there are billions of people in the world and you might see problems out there that seem insurmountable—but, I believe that small groups of people, or even an individual, can have an impact.

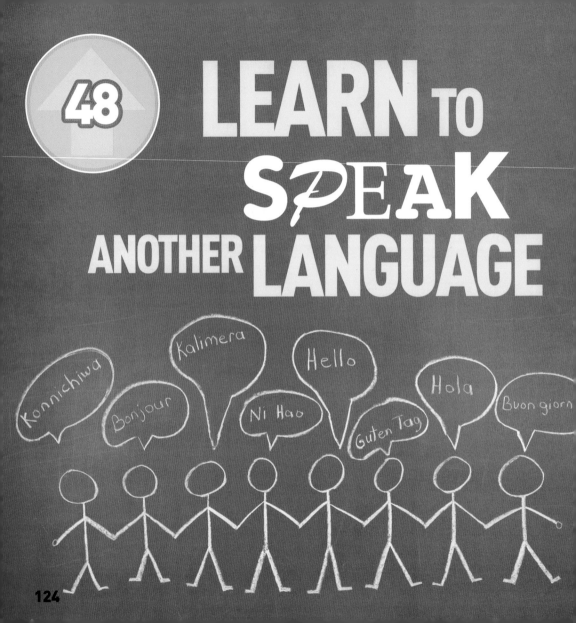

	Hello	**Goodbye**
French	Bonjour	Au revoir
Spanish	Hola	Adios
Italian	Ciao	Ciao
German	Hallo	Auf Wiedersehen
Mandarin Chinese	Ni hao	Zai jian

	Thank you	**I love you**
French	Merci	Je t'aime
Spanish	Gracias	Te amo
Italian	Grazie	Ti amo
German	Danke	Ich liebe dich
Mandarin Chinese	Xie xie ni	Wo ai ni

49

DISCOVER
YOUR HIDDEN
TALENT

Can you turn your EYELIDS INSIDE OUT?

Do a spot-on celebrity IMPERSONATION?

Maybe you've mastered the worm, or can WALK ON YOUR HANDS!

FIND SOMETHING you can do that's SPECIAL and UNIQUE (EVEN IF IT'S A BIT BIZARRE!).

50

DONATE
YOUR OLD CLOTHES AND TOYS

TO A CHARITABLE ORGANIZATION

Even clothes that are worn, torn, or stained can be recycled into things like polishing cloths, paper, seat stuffing, or car insulation.

When you donate the items you no longer need, you are not only giving them to people who could use them, you are also saving them from ending up in our already stuffed landfills. It's a win-win!

51

BAKE
SOMETHING
FROM
SCRATCH

CHEW ON THIS

make your own CUPCAKES!

 Heat the oven to 350°F. Line 12 muffin cups with paper liners.

 Beat 1 cup of butter, 1½ cups of sugar, 1 cup of unsweetened cocoa powder, 1 teaspoon of baking powder, ½ teaspoon of baking soda, and ¼ teaspoon of salt in a large bowl with a mixer for 1 minute.

 Add 2 large eggs and beat them for 2 minutes. Beat in 1 cup of milk and 2 teaspoons of vanilla, then add 2½ cups of flour.

 Spoon about ¼ cup of batter into each muffin cup, filling each about ⅔ full. Bake them for 20 to 25 minutes.

 Repeat step 4 with the remaining batter. Let the cupcakes cool for 5 minutes before frosting.

FLY A KITE

In the 1820s, an English schoolteacher and inventor, George Pocock, fastened two kites to a buggy. The force of the wind on the kite pulled the buggy along at almost 20 miles an hour (32 km/h).

PREPARE A PICNIC AND FIND THE PERFECT SPOT TO ENJOY IT.

HERE'S A SIMPLE RECIPE FROM
NATIONAL GEOGRAPHIC EXPLORER
AND CHEF BARTON SEAVER

Barton Seaver

Picnic-Perfect
Chicken Salad Sandwich
Yield: 4 servings
Prep time: About 1 hour

1 ¼ pound chicken breast, boneless and skinless
water
salt
4 tablespoons mayonnaise
2 tablespoons fresh tarragon (or 3 tablespoons dried tarragon)
1 cup green or red seedless grapes, sliced in half
8 slices whole wheat toast

Place the chicken in a small pot just big enough to hold it. Fill the pot with cold water and place over medium heat. As soon as the water begins to bubble, reduce the heat to low and let cook for approximately 15 minutes, or until the chicken is cooked to 165°F measured with a thermometer. Remove from heat and drain off the liquid.

When the chicken is cooled, cut it into small pieces and place in a bowl. Add the mayonnaise, tarragon, and grapes and stir to combine. Let the mixture sit for ten minutes for the flavors to combine. Serve on toasted bread and enjoy!

Excerpted from The National Geographic Kids' Cookbook

54

Steve Jobs reportedly proposed the name "Apple Computers" after returning from a visit to an apple farm. He said "it sounded fun, spirited, and not intimidating."

READ A BIOGRAPHY
(OR AUTOBIOGRAPHY) OF SOMEONE YOU ADMIRE

Can you think of a person who inspires or fascinates you? Find out more about them! Biographies (books about a person written by someone else) and autobiographies (books about a person written by that person) are chock-full of interesting details about their life, work, and personal experiences that outsiders usually don't know. By learning how that person thinks, feels, and what they've experienced, you begin to understand how they became who they are or were—and maybe you'll discover a little something about yourself along the way! Here are a few worth checking out...

Anne Frank: Diary of a Young Girl, by Anne Frank

Long Walk to Freedom, by Nelson Mandela

Into the Wild, by Jon Krakauer

Life in the Ocean: The Story of Oceanographer Sylvia Earle, by Claire A. Nivola

My Life With the Chimpanzees, by Jane Goodall

Dreams From My Father: A Story of Race and Inheritance, by President Barack Obama

VISIT A ZOO, AN AQUARIUM, AND A MUSEUM

—AND TAKE PICTURES
(if you're allowed)

TRY TO SNAP A PHOTO OF EACH OF THE FOLLOWING:

1 You on the front steps, or near the entrance.

2 The biggest piece of art, animal, artifact, or exhibit you saw, and the smallest.

3 Something you hadn't known, but learned about that day.

4 A piece of art, animal, artifact, or exhibit you want to learn more about.

5 Your favorite exhibit.

56

MAKE A LIST OF
10 THINGS

YOU LIKE ABOUT YOURSELF

(THEN READ IT WHENEVER YOU'RE FEELING DOWN.)

143

57

START
YOUR OWN
BUSINESS

TIPS

HERE ARE FIVE IDEAS TO GET YOU GOING:

- DOG WALKING
- LEMONADE STAND
- CAR WASH
- LAWN MOWING
- WINDOW WASHING

When Leanna Archer was just nine years old, she began packaging and selling a hair product made by her grandmother. Today, her business, Leanna's Hair, features a line of organic products sold throughout the United States.

58

CATCH LIGHTNING BUGS

MAKE A HOMEMADE LANTERN by putting them in a jar with holes poked in the top (but then be sure to release them at the end of the night!).

Also called fireflies, these insects are actually beetles. They take in oxygen and, inside special cells, combine it with a substance called luciferin to produce light with almost no heat.

BE AN
EXPLORER

MEET
ZEB HOGAN

AS AN AQUATIC ECOLOGIST, ZEB STUDIES UNDERWATER BIOLOGY AND SPECIFICALLY, HE WORKS TO SAVE CRITICALLY ENDANGERED FISH AND LEARN MORE ABOUT THEIR HABITATS.

ZEB HOGAN

On traveling to Cambodia in an effort to protect megafish, such as the Mekong giant catfish from local nets:

" The first year, we had one that weighed 595 pounds (270 kg). Bugs were swarming all around my headlamp, and someone pulled on a rope and this huge fish came out of the murk ... When we released the fish, it nearly sank us. Now we use bigger boats, but that night it was a 12-foot (3.7-m) boat dragging a 10-foot (3-m) fish. We inched along, killed the engine, and I jumped in. Giant catfish grow weak after fighting a net, and I have to grab on to them to make sure they're strong enough to swim before we release them. "

WANT TO BE AN
AQUATIC ECOLOGIST?

STUDY:
Ecology and biology

READ:
World Without Fish,
by Mark Kurlansky

WATCH:

Monster Fish
with Zeb Hogan

DO:

Volunteer at a
local aquarium to
discover more about
fish conservation.

Explore your
backyard, your
neighborhood, or
anyplace else that's
new to you. Get in
there, get curious,
and really take
a look!

iDeAS

MAKE AN INSPIRATION BOARD

Cut out words and pictures from magazines or news-papers of people, places, and ideas that inspire you. Include goals you want to accomplish. These can be any-thing, like: Travel to India! Be healthy! Get all A's next semester! Learn to do a wheelie on my bike! Be nicer to my sister! Then, put your board somewhere you can see it, as a daily reminder of what you're working toward.

61

LEARN SIGN LANGUAGE

The American Sign Language Alphabet

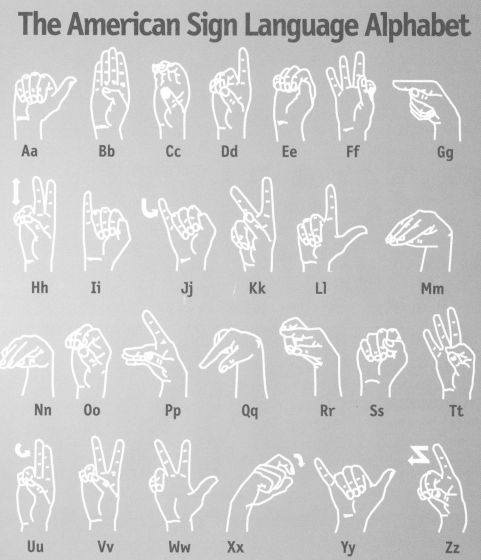

Aa Bb Cc Dd Ee Ff Gg

Hh Ii Jj Kk Ll Mm

Nn Oo Pp Qq Rr Ss Tt

Uu Vv Ww Xx Yy Zz

62

ORGANIZE A SCAVENGER HUNT

→ Gather your friends and split into two teams.

→ Ask one person (a parent or friend) to be the timekeeper and judge.

→ Each team makes a list of ten things for the other team to find in your house, backyard, or neighborhood (or use the list below).

→ Spend 15 minutes finding as many things on the list as you can.

→ Present your findings to the other team and the judge.

→ The team that found the most items on the list wins!

SAMPLE SCAVENGER HUNT LIST:

☑ A nut from a tree

☑ A food that can be eaten hot or cold

☑ Something squishy

☑ An animal that stands on two legs

☑ A picture of someone you've never met

☑ A toy or game that two people can play at once

☑ Something that makes music

☑ A piece of sporting equipment

☑ A book with an illustration on the cover

☑ Something that grows and has to be trimmed

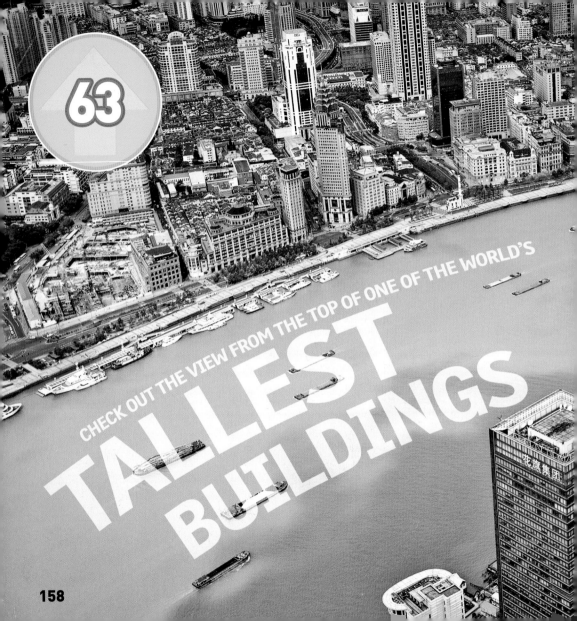

63

CHECK OUT THE VIEW FROM THE TOP OF ONE OF THE WORLD'S

TALLEST BUILDINGS

花旗集团

In hot weather, the metal on the Eiffel Tower expands, causing it to "grow" about six inches (152 mm).

MIRAE ASSET

BUILD A SANDCASTLE

HERE ARE FIVE TIPS FOR BUILDING A KILLER SANDCASTLE
FROM AWARD-WINNING SAND SCULPTOR AND AUTHOR OF
SANDCASTLES MADE SIMPLE, LUCINDA WIERENGA

The wetter the sand, the better. For the best sand, dig a hole near the water's edge. When you reach water, mix it with the sand and use that to build. Bonus: As wet sand settles, it naturally compacts, getting rid of excess air.

Try hand stacking. It's a technique in which you take handfuls of wet sand, flatten them like pancakes and stack them to create a tall tower.

Carve into the stack to create your castle's shape, working from the top to the bottom. Want to make a staircase? First build a ramp, then make a series of vertical and horizontal cuts to create the stairs.

Get creative with your tools. To smooth, etch, and carve the surfaces of your sculpture, you can use paint scrapers, spatulas, plastic utensils, or even shells that you find on the beach.

Experiment with forms. A form is something that will hold the sand as you compact it. Try cutting the bottom off of a bucket (or even a large plastic soda cup) and filling it with sand and water. Then gently tap the sides and lift the form. Now you should have a nice, compacted chunk of sand to work with.

160

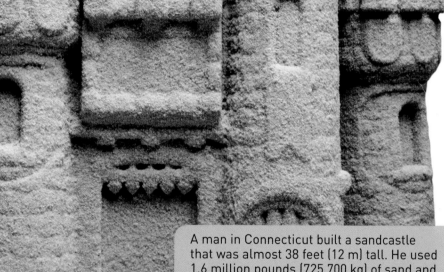

64

A man in Connecticut built a sandcastle that was almost 38 feet (12 m) tall. He used 1.6 million pounds (725,700 kg) of sand and water, 1,400 people helped him to build the castle, and it took 3,000 hours.

Groundhogs are sometimes called whistle-pigs because of a loud, high-pitched whistle they emit when they're alarmed.

LEARN TO WHISTLE

66

PERFORM

When William Shakespeare's plays were first performed in the late 1500s, women were not allowed to appear on stage, so men played all of the parts—both male and female.

ON A
STAGE

Many famous folks are also collectors. For instance, Dr. Seuss collected hats, Taylor Swift collects old bottles, and Tom Hanks collects vintage typewriters.

START A COLLECTION

IT CAN BE STAMPS, COINS, ROCKS, ACTION FIGURES, DOLLS, SNOW GLOBES, HAIR BALLS—ANYTHING!

GO
SNORKELING

Snorkels are just the right length for comfortable breathing under, but near, the surface of the water.

NOWHERE NEAR THE OCEAN? THROW ON A MASK AND SOME FINS AND **TAKE A DIP** IN A LOCAL POOL. **PRACTICE BREATHING UNDERWATER, ADJUSTING** YOUR MASK, AND **CLEARING WATER** FROM YOUR **SNORKEL.**

69

CONQUER A FEAR

When you encounter something really scary, your—as well as every other animal's—brain releases chemicals to help your body prepare for what's called "fight or flight." Among other things, your heart rate increases, your muscles tense up, your pupils dilate, and your brain becomes very focused on the task at hand.

> You gain strength, courage, and confidence by every experience in which you really stop to look fear in the face ... You must do the thing you think you cannot do.
> —Eleanor Roosevelt

SOME FEAR IS HEALTHY——it alerts us to situations that might be dangerous, like petting a bear, being outside in a lightning storm, or climbing too far from the ground. But sometimes we become afraid of things that are actually quite safe and could even be good (and fun!) for us, like going to the doctor, jumping off the high dive, or speaking in public! In these cases, it's really healthy to take steps to conquer the fears. Remember, bravery doesn't mean you aren't afraid, it means facing the things that scare you.

1 **WRITE YOUR FEAR DOWN.** The first step in fighting a fear is admitting it scares you.

2 **ENLIST SUPPORT.** Tell your parents, a sibling, or a friend what you're trying to do. Often having someone to talk to—and somebody cheering you on!—can be very helpful.

3 **MAKE A PLAN.** Decide how you're going to tackle this fear and do a little every day. If you're scared of dogs, you don't have to immediately interact with one. You can start just by looking at pictures of dogs or watching videos of dogs playing. The more you get used to seeing them, the less scary they'll seem. Then, work your way up to being around a dog that's on a leash or in a crate. Pretty soon, you'll be ready to let a dog sniff your hand or maybe even pet it.

4 **KEEP AT IT.** No matter what, don't give up. You can do it!

5 **BE KIND TO YOURSELF.** The things we say to ourselves, about ourselves, is called "self-talk." When trying to face a fear, it's important that our self-talk be positive and kind. For example: "I might not have been able to jump off the high dive today, but I am really trying and I will get there soon."

70

BE A TEAM PLAYER

JOIN A CLUB, A GROUP, OR AN ATHLETIC TEAM. No matter what you're interested in, it's a great way to meet new friends, keep your body and mind busy, and—hey—it beats rushing home from school to do homework any day!

71

TRY A POGO STICK

The term "Hula-Hooping" came from British sailors who had seen hula dancing in the Hawaiian islands and thought the movement looked similar to the exercises they had been doing using hoops.

HULA-HOP

JUMP ROPE

THESE OLD-TIMEY TOYS HAVEN'T BEEN AROUND FOREVER FOR NOTHING!

72

MAKE UP A

SCARY STORY

AND MASTER THE ART OF TELLING IT

(Preferably in a dark room with a flashlight!)

RECONNECT

WITH

AN OLD FRIEND

COMPLETE A PUZZLE

WITH 500 PIECES OR MORE

LOOKING FOR THE PERFECT CROWD-PLEASER?

75

IF YOU LIKE...	CHECK OUT...
MYSTERIES, SUSPENSEFUL STORIES, LOGIC	CLUE
BUSINESS, REAL ESTATE	MONOPOLY
BEING ACTIVE, GETTING SILLY	TWISTER
DRAWING, TEAMS, AND RACING AGAINST A CLOCK	PICTIONARY
HIGH INTENSITY, WORD GAMES, AND TEAMS	TABOO

76

SOLVE A MYSTERY

ARE YOU THE NEXT
SHERLOCK HOLMES OR
VERONICA MARS?

Try your hand at supersleuthing with these FIVE MYSTERY-SOLVING steps:

STEP 1: Identify suspects. Make a list of anyone who might be involved, as well as possible explanations for what occurred.

STEP 2: Gather clues. Get a pen and paper and write down all of the evidence. Use your five senses—sight, smell, touch, taste, hearing—and pay very close attention to details.

STEP 3: Narrow your focus. Go through your suspect list and remove anyone who couldn't have had something to do with the mystery.

STEP 4: Play out the possibilities. Now, put it all together—how would the various suspects have contributed to the evidence you collected? What might have happened and caused the mysterious circumstances?

STEP 5: Considering the suspicious scenario, the evidence you collected, and the suspects, draw a conclusion.

77

The cuckoo bird lays its eggs in the nest of another bird—one of a different species. The other bird then sits on the egg and takes care of the baby cuckoo when it hatches.

MAKE A
BIRD FEEDER

Hang it near a window, then identify the birds that come to eat.

There are several easy ways to make a bird feeder.

MILK CARTON:

- With scissors, CUT A SQUARE HOLE IN ONE SIDE of an empty milk carton.

- Poke a hole in the top of the carton and TIE A LARGE KNOT IN A PIECE OF STRING.

- THREAD THE STRING THROUGH THE BOTTOM OF THE HOLE, so that the knot is inside the carton and holding firmly.

- POUR BIRDSEED IN THE BOTTOM of the carton, up to the opening.

PLASTIC BOTTLE:

- Clean an empty one-liter soda bottle and CUT FOUR HOLES (two sets directly opposite one another, about two and four inches [5 and 10 cm] from the bottom).

- Put two wooden spoons through the holes (for the birds to stand on) and FILL THE BOTTLE WITH BIRDSEED.

- You can TIE TWINE AROUND THE NECK OF THE BOTTLE, or put a small eye screw through the plastic cap and loop twine through it.

PINECONE:

- Tie a string around a pinecone and SPREAD PEANUT BUTTER ALL OVER IT, making sure to get it between each of the scales.

- Then, put birdseed in the bottom of a tray or shallow dish and ROLL THE PINECONE IN THE SEEDS.

- You can also PRESS THE BIRDSEED INTO THE PEANUT BUTTER so that more sticks.

LEARN HOW TO TAKE A GREAT PHOTO

78

BECCA SKINNER,

23, is a National Geographic young explorer grantee and professional photographer. Here, she shares what she loves about her art, as well as her expert tips so that you can upgrade your photo skills from average to awesome.

Becca Skinner

PHOTOGRAPHY IS ... *a really cool way to tell a story to a large audience in a really artistic and tangible way.*

I MOST LIKE TO PHOTOGRAPH ... *outdoor adventure, social-justice-related subjects, and people.*

PHOTOGRAPHY HAS TAUGHT ME ... *that everyone has an important story to tell.*

THE COOLEST PLACE I'VE TAKEN PICTURES IS...

Sumatra, Indonesia. It's where I went with my Explorer's grant and it was the first time I traveled out of the country.

THE PHOTOGRAPHERS THAT I MOST ADMIRE ARE... *Jimmy Chin and Lynsey Addario.*

THE ELEMENTS THAT MAKE A GREAT PICTURE ARE... *the lighting and the emotion.*

TO TAKE A GREAT PICTURE... *don't always shoot standing up. Look low, look high—try to see the things that other people might overlook. Don't be afraid to change your perspective and try something different. Keep taking photos of one subject until you find an angle that you like. Often, the first photo that I take of something is not the one I like the best.*

TO BECOME A BETTER PHOTOGRAPHER... *shoot photographs often and get feedback.*

79

LIE IN A
HAMMOC

AND WATCH THE WORLD PASS BY

80

MEMORIZE ALL THE WORDS TO YOUR FAVORITE SONG,

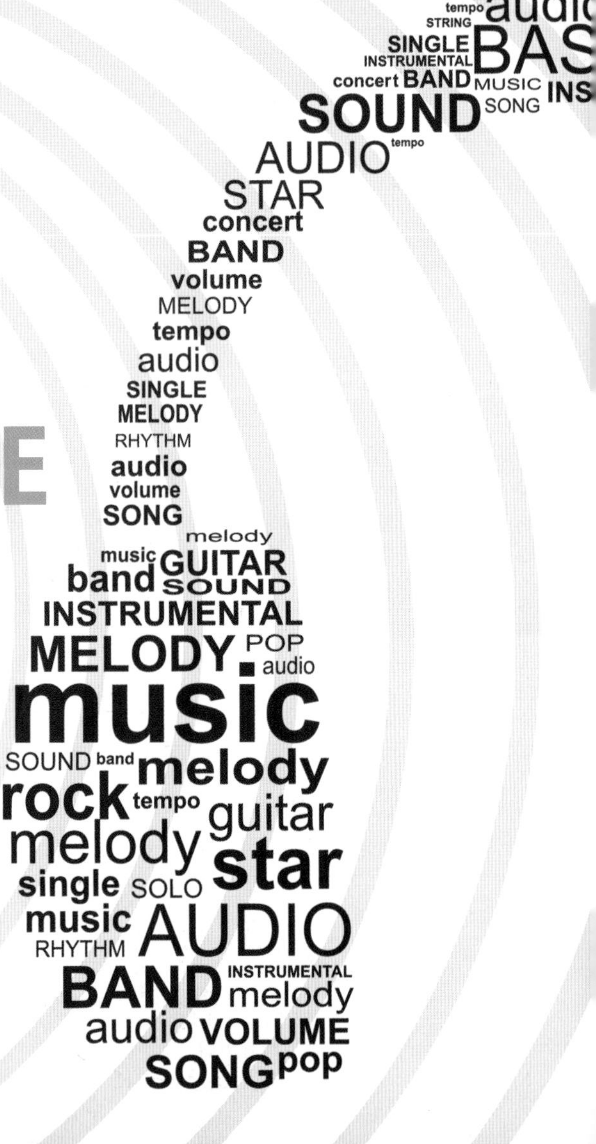

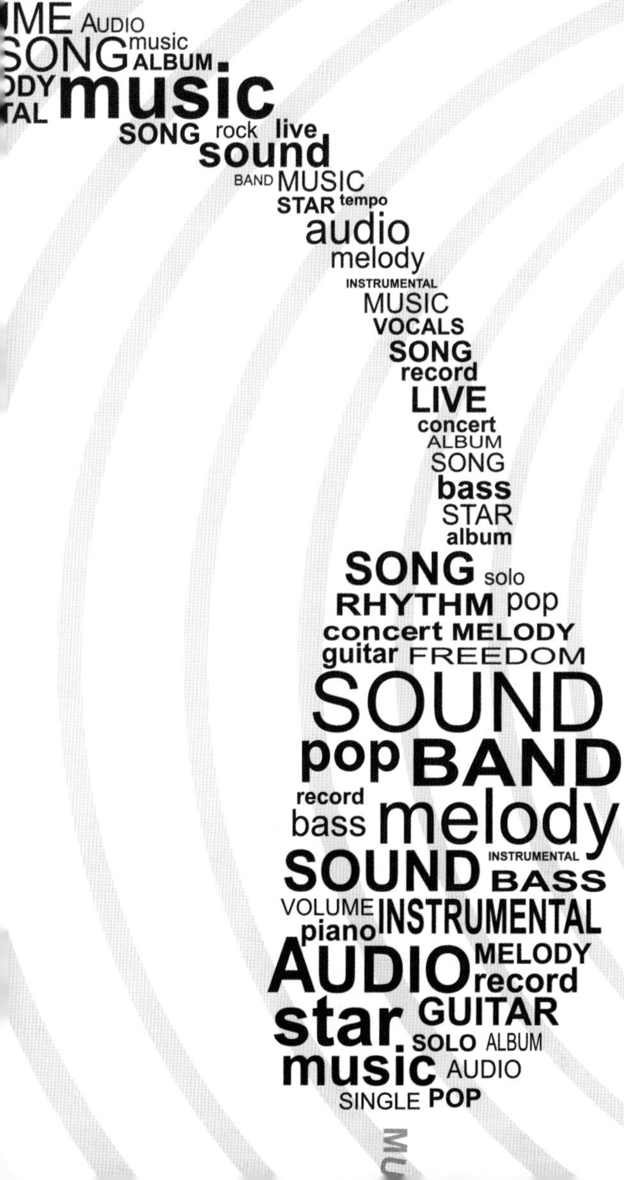

THEN BELT IT OUT WHEN IT COMES ON THE RADIO

CANOE, KAYAK, or FLOAT IN A TUBE DOWN A RIVER

LEARN TO DO A CARTWHEEL

MAKE AN
AWESOME
PAPER AIRPLANE

Get started with this simple plane, then tinker with adjustments to make it fly faster, longer, or in a straighter line.

 Fold a sheet of computer paper in half, vertically.

2. On one end, fold each corner toward the middle so that the inner edges touch the crease.

3. Starting at the tip in the center, fold each side down so that their inner edges touch the crease in the center of the paper.

4. Turn the airplane on its side and fold it in half along the centerline.

5. Now fold each wing, from the corner opposite the centerfold toward the bottom corner.

6. Hold your plane beneath its wings, pull your wrist back, then flick it forward and let go.

7. Hone your skills and challenge your friends to a paper airplane building contest. Don't tell them you've been practicing.

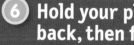

85

LEARN HOW TO PROPERLY SET THE TABLE

Other countries have different customs when it comes to mealtime. For example, in Chile it is considered rude to eat anything with your fingers—even french fries; in Japan it is considered polite, and flattering to the chef, to slurp your noodles; and in China it is rude to eat everything on your plate, as it's thought to imply that there wasn't enough food.

LIZZIE POST,
of the Emily Post Institute, explains

HOW TO PROPERLY SET THE TABLE

and share good mealtime manners.

THE (1) NAPKIN SHOULD BE PLACED UNDERNEATH, OR TO THE LEFT OF, THE (2) FORK; (3) PLATE; (4) KNIFE, WHICH SHOULD BE POSITIONED WITH THE BLADE FACING TOWARD THE PLATE; AND (5) SPOON. THE (6) GLASS SHOULD BE PLACED ABOVE THE KNIFE.

WHAT IF...	LIZZIE POST SAYS...
I just took a bite of my hamburger, but I have something really important to say?	Wait until you're done with that bite. You want to make sure your lips are closed whenever there's anything in your mouth.
I'm at a friend's house and I don't like what's being served?	As long as you're not allergic to it, take a tiny portion so that you can try it. We call this a "no thank you helping."
I need to use the restroom during dinner?	Ask, "May I please be excused to the restroom?" Then, place your napkin next to your plate, not on your chair.
I want something that's across the table from me?	If you would have to cross into someone else's space in order to reach it, ask whoever's closest to it to pass it to you. For example, "Would you please pass me the broccoli?"
I want to finish a game I'm playing on my phone.	You should put your phone away and focus on the people that you're with. Remember to participate in conversation. Dinner is really a time to connect—whether it's with your family or someone else's.

86 LOOK THROUGH A TELESCOPE AT THE NIGHT SKY

BE SURE TO CHECK OUT THE MOON!

In some parts of the world, it is thought that the light and dark areas on the surface of the moon (which are just high and low land surfaces) look like a man's face ("the man in the moon"). In other countries, they are thought to resemble a rabbit.

87

Master the art
OF A GREAT HANDSHAKE

STEP 1:

Look the person in the eyes.

STEP 2:

Use a firm grip (but not too firm—you're not arm wrestling!).

STEP 3:

Give two or three light shakes.

STEP 4:

Use the person's name.
For example:
Thank you for inviting me, Mrs. Burrell; or *It's great to meet you, Larry.*

STEP 5:

The handshake should only last a few seconds, then politely retract your hand and begin your conversation.

Depending on where you are in the world, it may be customary to greet someone by bowing, kissing on the cheeks, or even rubbing noses.

88

In 1911, the "Mona Lisa" was stolen from the Louvre in Paris by a museum employee and his two brothers. To carry off the heist, they hid in a closet overnight and then took the painting on a day when the museum was closed to visitors.

DISCOVER YOUR INNER PICASSO

5 ARTISTIC MASTERPIECES TO TRY

PAINT

a self-portrait

Mold something out of

CLAY

MAKE A COLLAGE

Draw an object on a piece of paper, then glue small, torn bits of colored paper to fill it in. You can use construction paper or even torn pages from magazines.

CREATE ABSTRACT ART

Abstract art uses colors, shapes, and lines to express a mood or feeling. It isn't meant to represent a specific object or scene, so often it's up to the viewer to interpret.

Draw a still life with

CHARCOAL

A still life is a picture of nonliving objects, like a bowl of fruit, an old chair, or a tea set.

89

HAVE A WATER BALLOON FIGHT

FIND YOUR LUCKY CHARM

BE ON THE LOOKOUT FOR THESE 10 SYMBOLS OF GOOD LUCK:

1. FOUR-LEAF CLOVER
2. SHOOTING STAR
3. HEADS-UP PENNY
4. RABBIT'S FOOT
5. WISHBONE
6. HORSESHOE
7. BAMBOO
8. LADYBUG
9. RAINBOW
10. NUMBER 7

CHECK OUT THE VIEW FROM INSIDE A FAMOUS BUILDING

The Statue of Liberty is more than 305 feet (93 m) tall. The length of just her index finger is 8 feet (2.4 m).

PICK A SPORT AND STICK WITH IT

INTERVIEW YOUR GRANDPARENTS

Though it may be hard to imagine, your grandma and grandpa had long, interesting lives before you came into the picture. They may have had some wild adventures even. And guess what? The older someone is, the better the stories. Chances are, if you take some time to ask your grandparents questions about their childhood, some of the answers might surprise you! Oh, and be sure to record it. You'll be glad you did one day.

> NOT SURE WHAT TO ASK?

Here are 10 questions to get your creativity flowing:

1 What was the toy you remember wanting most when you were little? Did you ever get it?

2 What invention has created the greatest change in your lifetime?

3 What was your house like growing up?

4 Did you like school when you were my age?

5 What were the popular fashions and hairstyles when you were my age?

6 What was the first concert you went to?

7 Did you take any family vacations when you were young? Where to? How did you get there?

8 What was your first job?

9 How did you meet Grandma/Grandpa?

10 What was my mom/dad like growing up?

STAY UP ALL

But not on a school night!

INVENT SOMETHING

Did you know that Popsicles, earmuffs, and the trampoline were all invented by kids? NOW IT'S YOUR TURN! Here are some tips for dreaming up the next big thing.

- **FIND A NEED.** Make a list of things in your everyday life that need fixing or improving. Does changing your cat's litter box get on your nerves? Do you hate how the side of your hand gets marker on it when you're coloring? Or, does it bother you when the bottoms of your pants get wet when it rains?

- **BRAINSTORM SOLUTIONS.** Now, think of ways to address the needs you've identified. Write down everything and anything you think of.

- **NARROW YOUR FOCUS.** Look over your list and pick your best idea.

- **RESEARCH MATERIALS.** Read all about products similar to the one you're envisioning. How were they made? What will you need to make your idea a reality?

- **BUILD IT.** Give it a try, and if it doesn't work, go back to the drawing board and try again!

Play-Doh was originally made to clean coal residue, or soot, from wallpaper, but since it resembled modeling clay and it wasn't messy or toxic, the creators quickly realized it made a great toy.

96

DISCOVER YOUR PERSONAL STYLE

TAVI GEVINSON,

17, started her fashion blog, Style Rookie, when she was 11 years old. Then, three years later, she founded *Rookie*, the amazing online magazine for teen girls.

Tavi Gevinson

Q: WHAT WAS IT THAT FIRST DREW YOU TO FASHION?

A: I think I was just bored of wearing the same thing. It seemed exciting to get to be a different character every day.

Q: WHAT DOES IT MEAN TO HAVE GREAT STYLE?

A: I like seeing people who wear what they want. That's the most fun way to be.

Q: HOW WOULD YOU DESCRIBE YOUR PERSONAL STYLE?

A: It changes a lot. I used to like dressing up like characters. Now, I want to wear things that feel more like me, which is something simple that I can work in and get messy. Lately I find myself wearing overalls every day.

Q: WHO ARE YOUR STYLE INFLUENCES?

A: Within three days of each other, I saw both Taylor Swift and Patti Smith in concert. That kind of summarizes the spectrum of how I want to dress. Taylor Swift wore really pretty dresses and theatrical outfits and Patti Smith was really relaxed and natural.

Q: DO YOU HAVE ANY STYLE RULES THAT YOU LIVE BY?

A: No rules. But, if I'm wearing something weird and I find myself second-guessing it as I'm about to leave the house, I force myself to wear it. I know now that it feels bad to come home from school and think, Oh I wish I had a bit more confidence this morning, I could have worn what I wanted. And it's fun to come home and feel like you conquered something that day.

Q: WHAT ADVICE WOULD YOU GIVE SOMEONE WHO IS JUST STARTING TO EXPLORE THEIR PERSONAL STYLE?

A: Don't be afraid of feeling goofy or drawing attention to yourself. Don't worry about what other people might say. I don't dress as colorfully as I did a few years ago, but when I look back at those photos, while I look totally goofy, I'd never been happier. That's the important thing: It's not really about how what you wear, looks—it's more about how it makes you feel.

97

TAKE BASIC FIRST AID FROM THE AMERICAN RED CROSS

FIRST AID

98

MAKE A VIDEO ABOUT SOMETHING IMPORTANT TO YOU

0:25:37   HD

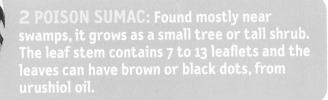

99
LEARN TO IDENTIFY THESE FIVE HARMFUL PLANTS

1 POISON IVY: It has solid green, pointed leaves that hang from the stem in groups of three. It contains an oil called urushiol that can cause an itchy, painful rash.

2 POISON SUMAC: Found mostly near swamps, it grows as a small tree or tall shrub. The leaf stem contains 7 to 13 leaflets and the leaves can have brown or black dots, from urushiol oil.

3 STINGING NETTLES: This plant has drooping, loosely hanging, oval, toothed leaves. It also has hair on its leaves and stem, which will sting you if you touch them.

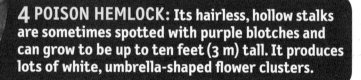

4 POISON HEMLOCK: Its hairless, hollow stalks are sometimes spotted with purple blotches and can grow to be up to ten feet (3 m) tall. It produces lots of white, umbrella-shaped flower clusters.

5 CACTUS: Cacti live in dry climates and have long, fleshy stems that store water. They are covered in very sharp (and sometimes long) spines. Some of their spines are barbed and therefore difficult to remove if they get stuck in your skin.

SEE THESE **5**

100

ALL-TIME CLASSIC MOVIES

(as voted by our very own NG Kids' readers!)

1
WILLY WONKA AND THE CHOCOLATE FACTORY

2
THE WIZARD OF OZ

3
HARRY POTTER AND THE SORCERER'S STONE

4
THE LION KING

5
THE SOUND OF MUSIC

CHECKLIST

- ☐ Do something nice for someone but don't tell them you did it
- ☐ Learn a joke and how to tell it
- ☐ Visit an orchard and pick your own fruit
- ☐ Climb a mountain
- ☐ Ride a roller coaster
- ☐ Become a pen pal
- ☐ Try yoga
- ☐ Rake leaves into a big pile and then jump in them
- ☐ Persuade your parents to make a change for the environment
- ☐ Record your dreams for a week
- ☐ Go camping
- ☐ Ride a horse
- ☐ Become an expert at something
- ☐ Step outside of your comfort zone
- ☐ Run a 5k
- ☐ Help someone in need
- ☐ Play in the mud
- ☐ Learn to play an instrument
- ☐ Try another country's cuisine
- ☐ Learn a dance
- ☐ Volunteer in your community
- ☐ Adopt an animal
- ☐ Read an entire book series
- ☐ Make homemade ice cream
- ☐ Go to a concert
- ☐ Learn how to sew on a button
- ☐ Catch a fish (and be sure to take a picture!)
- ☐ Go to a parade
- ☐ Write a letter to make a difference
- ☐ Experience a new way to travel
- ☐ Save enough money to buy something you've had your eye on
- ☐ Throw a backyard bash
- ☐ Plant a garden and watch it grow
- ☐ Attend a professional sporting event
- ☐ Ride a bike somewhere that you'd usually take a car
- ☐ Blow bubbles
- ☐ Swim in an ocean, lake, or stream
- ☐ Take a trip to a state that does not border your own
- ☐ Join the workforce (temporarily)
- ☐ Become a master public speaker
- ☐ Learn how to scramble an egg, make a grilled cheese sandwich, and ice a cake
- ☐ Make your own comic book
- ☐ Visit a working farm
- ☐ Learn about a religion other than your own
- ☐ Write a poem
- ☐ Watch a black-and-white movie
- ☐ Champion a cause you care about
- ☐ Learn to speak another language
- ☐ Discover your hidden talent
- ☐ Donate your old clothes and toys to a charitable organization
- ☐ Bake something from scratch
- ☐ Fly a kite

- [ ] Prepare a picnic and find the perfect spot to enjoy it
- [ ] Read a biography (or autobiography) of someone you admire
- [ ] Visit a zoo, an aquarium, and a museum —and take pictures
- [ ] Make a list of 10 things you like about yourself (then read it whenever you're feeling down)
- [ ] Start your own business
- [ ] Catch lightning bugs
- [ ] Be an explorer
- [ ] Make an inspiration board
- [ ] Learn sign language
- [ ] Organize a scavenger hunt
- [ ] Check out the view from the top of one of the world's tallest buildings
- [ ] Build a sandcastle
- [ ] Learn to whistle
- [ ] Perform on a stage
- [ ] Start a collection
- [ ] Go snorkeling
- [ ] Conquer a fear
- [ ] Be a team player
- [ ] Try a pogo stick, Hula-Hoop, and jump rope
- [ ] Make up a scary story and master the art of telling it
- [ ] Reconnect with an old friend
- [ ] Complete a puzzle with 500 pieces or more
- [ ] Host a board game night for your friends
- [ ] Solve a mystery
- [ ] Make a bird feeder
- [ ] Learn how to take a great photo
- [ ] Lie in a hammock and watch the world pass by
- [ ] Memorize all the words to your favorite song, then belt it out when it comes on the radio
- [ ] Canoe, kayak, or float in a tube down a river
- [ ] Learn to do a cartwheel
- [ ] Make an awesome paper airplane
- [ ] Build a fort
- [ ] Learn how to properly set the table
- [ ] Look through a telescope at the night sky
- [ ] Master the art of a great handshake
- [ ] Discover your inner Picasso
- [ ] Have a water balloon fight
- [ ] Find your lucky charm
- [ ] Check out the view from inside a famous building
- [ ] Pick a sport and stick with it
- [ ] Interview your grandparents
- [ ] Stay up all night
- [ ] Invent something
- [ ] Discover your personal style
- [ ] Take basic first aid from the American Red Cross
- [ ] Make a video about something important to you
- [ ] Learn to identify these five harmful plants
- [ ] See these five all-time classic movies

INDEX

Find Out More

Grab a parent and visit these websites for more information!

1. dosomething.org
2. emilypost.com
3. kids.nationalgeographic.com
4. melissadarabian.net
5. nationalgeographic.com
6. nautiluslive.org

PHOTO CREDITS

For my family, Larry, Gail, and Alison, who made growing up (and who make being a grown-up) the most fun. —LG

PUBLISHED BY THE NATIONAL GEOGRAPHIC SOCIETY

John M. Fahey, *Chairman of the Board and Chief Executive Officer*
Declan Moore, *Executive Vice President; President, Publishing and Travel*
Melina Gerosa Bellows, *Publisher; Chief Creative Officer, Books, Kids, and Family*

PREPARED BY THE BOOK DIVISION

Hector Sierra, *Senior Vice President and General Manager*
Nancy Laties Feresten, *Senior Vice President, Kids Publishing and Media*
Jennifer Emmett, *Vice President, Editorial Director, Kids Books*
Eva Absher-Schantz, *Design Director, Kids Publishing and Media*
Jay Sumner, *Director of Photography, Kids Publishing*
R. Gary Colbert, *Production Director*
Jennifer A. Thornton, *Director of Managing Editorial*

STAFF FOR THIS BOOK

Becky Baines, *Project Editor*
Kathryn Robbins, *Art Director*
Hillary Leo, *Associate Photo Editor*
Ariane Szu-Tu, *Editorial Assistant*
Callie Broaddus, *Design Production Assistant*
Margaret Leist, *Photo Assistant*
Cathleen Carey and Moriah Petty, *Editorial Interns*
Grace Hill, *Associate Managing Editor*
Joan Gossett, *Production Editor*
Lewis R. Bassford, *Production Manager*
Susan Borke, *Legal and Business Affairs*

PRODUCTION SERVICES

Phillip L. Schlosser, *Senior Vice President*
Chris Brown, *Vice President, NG Book Manufacturing*
George Bounelis, *Senior Production Manager*
Nicole Elliott, *Director of Production*
Rachel Faulise, *Manager*
Robert L. Barr, *Manager*

The National Geographic Society is one of the world's largest nonprofit scientific and educational organizations. Founded in 1888 to "increase and diffuse geographic knowledge," the Society's mission is to inspire people to care about the planet. It reaches more than 400 million people worldwide each month through its official journal, *National Geographic*, and other magazines; National Geographic Channel; television documentaries; music; radio; films; books; DVDs; maps; exhibitions; live events; school publishing programs; interactive media; and merchandise. National Geographic has funded more than 10,000 scientific research, conservation, and exploration projects and supports an education program promoting geographic literacy.

For more information, please visit nationalgeographic.com, call 1-800-NGS LINE (647-5463), or write to the following address:
National Geographic Society
1145 17th Street N.W.
Washington, D.C. 20036-4688 U.S.A.

Visit us online at nationalgeographic.com/books

For librarians and teachers: ngchildrensbooks.org

More for kids from National Geographic:
kids.nationalgeographic.com

For information about special discounts for bulk purchases, please contact National Geographic Books Special Sales: ngspecsales@ngs.org

For rights or permissions inquiries, please contact National Geographic Books Subsidiary Rights: ngbookrights@ngs.org

Paperback ISBN: 978-1-4263-1558-9
Reinforced library binding ISBN: 978-1-4263-1611-1

Printed in the United States of America

14/QGT-CML/1

5445 9776 06/14

Neither the publisher nor the author shall be liable for any bodily harm that may be caused or sustained as a result of conducting any of the activities described in this book.